Your Thoughts Create Your World

Learn how to create the life you want by taking charge of your self-talk.

Anyone can understand and master this key to the good life. But hold on, it may change your entire life.

~

Don Steckdaub PhD

BALBOA.
PRESS

A DIVISION OF HAY HOUSE

Balboa Press books may be ordered through booksellers or by contacting:

Balboa Press
A Division of Hay House
1663 Liberty Drive
Bloomington, IN 47403
www.balboapress.com
1-(877) 407-4847

Because of the dynamic nature of the Internet, any web addresses or
links contained in this book may have changed since publication and
may no longer be valid. The views expressed in this work are solely those
of the author and do not necessarily reflect the views of the publisher,
and the publisher hereby disclaims any responsibility for them.

The author of this book does not dispense medical advice or prescribe the use
of any technique as a form of treatment for physical, emotional, or medical
problems without the advice of a physician, either directly or indirectly. The
intent of the author is only to offer information of a general nature to help
you in your quest for emotional and spiritual well-being. In the event you use
any of the information in this book for yourself, which is your constitutional
right, the author and the publisher assume no responsibility for your actions.

Any people depicted in stock imagery provided by Thinkstock are models,
and such images are being used for illustrative purposes only.
Certain stock imagery © Thinkstock.

ISBN: 978-1-4525-4524-0 (sc)
ISBN: 978-1-4525-4525-7 (e)
Library of Congress Control Number: 2012900144
Printed in the United States of America

Balboa Press rev. date:2/2/2012

Preface

For nearly forty years I have worked in the counseling field. During that time I have tasked myself to find a way to describe how individuals, couples, families and institutions, function well and how they dysfunction. I have read many books, studied many philosophies and religions, attended schools and seminars, talked with, and to, thousands of people. I have studied Twelve Step approaches, created a successful business, loved much, and married well.

This chip of a book is my attempt to impart what I have distilled from my life experiences both personally and professionally. I have a passion to share what I have learned and experienced in the hope that others might find the high road and be able to create a life they identify as good and rewarding.

I owe gratitude to many people. Everyone I have met has been a teacher. To name only a few is not fair, but necessary. Three people have had a profound influence on my thinking; Dr. Herbert Beierle, Dr. Albert Ellis, and "Chuck" Chamberlin. Many more have given me ideas and challenged me to think. Among my best teachers have been my mother, my children, and my wife, Rita. I thank them all.

Special thanks are offered to my longtime friend and colleague, Claudia Black for her support and to my daughter Cynthia Coleman for her editing and constant encouragement. Rita, thank you for your inspiration, encouragement and support.

Self Talk / Thinking

Thinking is only the process of talking to oneself.

Unknown

Life consists in what a man is thinking of all day.

Ralph Waldo Emerson

The soul of God is poured into the world through the thoughts of men.

Ralph Waldo Emerson

Beauty is no quality in things themselves: It exists merely in the mind which contemplates them.

David Hume

The glow of one warm thought is to me worth more than money.

Thomas Jefferson

Our life always expresses the result of our dominant thoughts.

Soren Kirkegaard

If we examine our thoughts, we shall find them always occupied with the past and the future.

Blaise Pascal

Thinking: talking of the soul with itself.

Plato

Thought takes man out of servitude, into freedom.

Henry Wadsworth Longfellow

Most people would die rather than think; in fact they do.

Bertrand Russell

All that we are is the result of what we have thought. The mind is everything. What we think, we become.

Buddha

Thought is parent of the deed.

Thomas Carlyle

He who would be useful strong and happy must cease to be a passive receptacle for the negative, beggarly and impure streams of thought; and as a wise householder commands his servants and invites his guests, so must he learn to command his desires and to say, with authority, what thoughts he shall admit into the mansion of his soul.

James Allen

THE SELF-TALK TRIANGLE

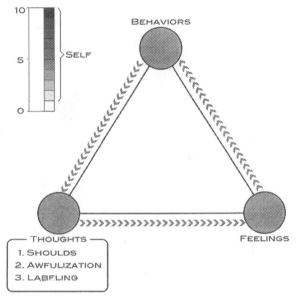

CHANGE YOUR THOUGHTS ~ CHANGE YOUR LIFE

The Self-Talk Triangle Explained

Let's look at the Self-Talk Triangle (Figure 1) to see if we can understand how our thoughts, feelings and behaviors are connected. Individuals and couples have benefitted from this material; I have shared it with thousands of people in church and workshops. These concepts have been taught in groups of all kinds: anger management, parenting, child batterers, spousal abuse perpetrators, convicted sex offenders, and substance abuse groups helping alcoholics and addicts of all kinds.

I have yet to find anyone who does not understand the Self-Talk Triangle when explained. The concept describes the process used by every human being. This is the simplest way I know to explain how people function and dysfunction. Stay open minded and see if this applies to you and everyone you know.

Thoughts create feelings

Plato is reported to have said, "People think, feel, and do." People have thoughts, feelings, and behaviors. The thoughts I hold in my head (my Self-Talk) tend to create the feelings I experience. Feelings come from somewhere; they don't drop out of a passing cloud. I believe we create our feelings by what we listen to on our Self-Talk Tape.

Let's try a typical example. If I have thoughts of anger and I listen to those thoughts all day, I will feel angry. If I have thoughts of depression, I will create corresponding feelings of depression. How could I not? If I listen to positive thoughts of peace, hope, love, and kindness, I will create feelings that are much more desirable.

If we create the feelings we experience, would we not want to create feelings of peace, joy, success and happiness? Happy, Joyous, and Free is the goal of thousands of people in recovery. Discovering that I have created feelings from the thoughts I have been listening to, where does the Triangle take me next?

Feelings dictate behaviors

The feelings *I create* dictate the behaviors I experience throughout the day. If I have created angry feelings by listening to angry thoughts on my Self-Talk Tape, I will, without a doubt, act that anger out during the day. I may find myself yelling at the idiots on the freeway or giving them the one finger salute. I may be grouchy and quick to anger.

If I have created feelings of depression, I am sure to act those feelings out. When I wake up I may pull the covers back over my head. I may call in sick, again. I may devour a package of Oreo cookies or other comfort food. Or, I may choose to get drunk and try to drown my woes.

The same is true if I listen to uplifting and life-affirming thoughts. I will behave in a way that exhibits those feelings. The positive uplifting feelings I experience will be evident to me and to everyone around me. I will probably smile more, be more tolerant of others, and have a chance of thoroughly enjoying my day.

I believe it is all important to monitor the thoughts I allow to remain on my Self-Talk Tape because they create my feelings, my behaviors, and therefore my life.

Behaviors reinforce thoughts

The behaviors I display (how I act) throughout the day tend to reinforce the thoughts I listen to all day. If I act angry it reinforces the angry thoughts on my Self-Talk Tape. I may tell myself how badly others have treated me, how I never get a break, that I am in a bad marriage and have a rotten job. I gather evidence to justify the feelings I have and the behaviors I exhibit.

However, if I act with kindness, patience, and tolerance of others, then those thoughts are reinforced. Life seems much more pleasant. I can take the hard knocks when they come with more grace and ease.

The cycle of thoughts, feelings, and behaviors never stops. The good news is, I can change my thoughts and consequently change my life. It is freeing to recognize this truth. It may also be a bit scary if this is the first time I have been told that I am responsible for the thoughts I entertain, for the feelings I create, and for the behaviors I display.

It is all up to me. I have the power to create the life I want to experience. I can load my tape with thoughts of joy and happiness or I can allow negative destructive thoughts to create pain, unhappiness, and disharmony.

Three Destructive Thought Patterns

The Shoulds

There are three primary thought patterns that cause the most trouble. The first occurs when I allow a lot of *should* statements to poison my thinking and create feelings and behaviors that I don't want to experience. This has been referred to as the, "tyranny of the shoulds."

I listen to the messages on my Self-Talk Tape throughout the day. When I am constantly telling myself exactly how everything and everybody *should* be, I set myself up for great emotional pain. And, the more rigid I become in how people, things, and events must be, the more frustrated I make myself. Here is the key. Life does not operate on my *shoulds*. When I demand that you, the government, other people, or the courts etc., operate according to my *shoulds* I make myself and everyone around me miserable.

This becomes a major problem when I let my *shoulds* turn into Musts or Have Tos, when I allow my demands to become dictatorial and demanding. For example, "They should see it my way. They must treat me better. They have to respect me and do it my way."

When we impose our *shoulds* on other people we create problems. Let me share an example. I was traveling on the freeway between two of our treatment facilities to conduct a men's anger management group. Glancing in my rear view mirror I saw a motorcycle speeding up behind me extremely fast. As the motorcycle passed me, I saw that it was one of my group members. He saw me at the same time I saw him.

When I arrived at the group, the motorcycle rider was sitting in his seat with a big grin. I asked him, "Brian, what were you doing out there?" He replied, "I was going about a hundred and twenty five, but it is no big deal. I go everywhere fast. People **should** just get out of my way and let me go. I'm not hurting anyone." That is his **should**.

An older man in group quickly stated, "No son, that's not how it works. People **should** drive the speed limit. That's what is safe and legal. When I see someone coming up behind me like that, I pull in front of him and slow down." At that moment I was glad these two individuals met in group and not out on the freeway.

This is a core issue of all relationship problems. This is true with personal relationships among family members, work associates and in society as a whole. It is also true in national and international relations. One does not need to look far to see evidence of this. If I believe an issue or situation **should**, **must** or **has to** be my way, that I am right and others are wrong, there will be no peace. Peace resides in the heart of the one who wears his/her beliefs like a loose robe and does not put on a suit of armor to defend their rigidly held beliefs.

The big problem comes when I become rigid in my **shoulds** and do not allow tolerance for other people's views and beliefs. I see this frequently with couples who come to me for marriage (or divorce) counseling. The husband has developed rigid views of how their marriage **should** or **must** work. The wife may have equally rigid views. When they do not compromise, all that is left is head-butting with each partner insisting they are right and the other is wrong.

Tolerance and patience is needed as a new way of communicating is developed and practiced. If the couple is not willing to work for a win-win outcome, they will both lose.

Look at the world at large. We see the leaders of nations dig in their heels and insist that everything be their way. They put their nation at war to defend their rigid, unyielding beliefs. The Self-Talk of leaders in power can bring about peace and harmony or it can create pain, panic, and disharmony.

When applying these principles, it does not mean that I need to become totally passive and deny my preferences. It does mean I need to improve my communication skills and to become a good listener who is skilled at voicing my opinions and preferences in such a way that my partner will listen. These skills can be worked on for a lifetime.

Before I leave a discussion of the ***shoulds***, let me warn you about another trap. We can ***should*** on other people harshly but we can ***should*** on ourselves in the same way. We can be merciless on ourselves. "I ***should*** have a better job, home, marriage, education, or car. I ***should*** be taller, thinner, prettier, smarter, etc. And, because I don't meet my ***should*** requirements, for example, I'm not as good as the next guy or gal, I'm a Zero. I don't like me and I won't let you like me either." Our ***shoulds*** need to be recognized, challenged, and changed.

Let's be clear. The messages we listen to may have originated with others when they were describing their world and how everything ***should*** be. They pass these messages along thinking they are teaching us how to get along in the world and how to take care of ourselves. These messages are reinforced as we listen to the opinions of others.

We need to risk <u>thinking for our selves</u> and changing the beliefs and Self-Talk that does not bring joy, peace and happiness to our lives and to the lives of those we love.

Let's move to the second big offender to creating the joy and happiness I would like to experience.

Awfulization

The second big offender is a word coined by Albert Ellis that I find very helpful in describing how people sabotage their efforts to find joy, happiness, and harmony with others. *Awfulization* occurs when we encounter a problem or challenge that we regard as an unsolvable, irreparable, and insurmountable tragic event.

Let me share a story that illustrates ***awfulization***. A man was referred to my office, by the court, for spousal battery. He seemed angry and confused. He told me that he considered himself a good husband who loved his wife and family very much. He was a hard worker. He told me he always turned his paycheck over to his wife and that he provided her with a nice home, a car, a refrigerator, and everything she needed. He was very proud of himself as a husband and provider.

However, there was one thing missing. Because he worked hard and returned home each evening tired and hungry, she ***should*** always have dinner on the table, the house clean, and the children quiet. That was how it was in his father's home, and his grandfather's and it ***should*** be that way in his home as well, "I have told her over and over how it ***must*** be." His wife would comply with his wishes

11

sometimes, but sometimes he would come home to a house in disarray and no dinner on the table.

One night several weeks prior, he came home tired and found no dinner on the table, and the house and children had not been tended to. He started an argument with his wife, letting her know how angry he was. He had a few beers which didn't help. The argument erupted again and, out of frustration, he slapped her. The neighbors heard the loud argument and called the police. When the police came they arrested him and charged him with spousal abuse. While he spent time in jail he lost his job and his wife threatened divorce. He had a legitimate problem. He was unhappy at home and felt he was not being respected or getting his needs met. Now, this is what I call *awfulizing* a problem. He took a situation in which he was unhappy, a level Two problem and escalated it into a level Ten problem that caused him and his family great pain. *Awfulizing* a problem is an inadequate and ineffective substitute for working with the other person to reach an amicable resolution.

Refer to the scale in the upper left hand corner of the diagram of the Self-Talk Triangle (Figure 1a). He, all by himself, took this problem from a One or a Two to a Ten with no help whatsoever. He *awfulized* the problem right off the scale. The scale demonstrates how a legitimate level Two or Three problem can be magnified all by our selves. Each action taken by the man in the story moved the seriousness of the problem to a new level.

I think it is fair to say we human beings are prone to taking small problems and concerns and making them into something unmanageable. We have all had that experience. We pay a price when we get into this habit. As I explain this concept to my court-referred clients they often remark, "Wow, that is how I got into this mess in the first place."

Labeling

This is the third area where we sabotage our attempts to create a peaceful and rewarding life. When people are not behaving the way we think they should, it is easy to start *labeling* them as no good. When institutions do not do it the way we think they should, it is easy to put a *label* on them. They are too liberal or too conservative. They are corrupt or out to get me.

Using the example in the scenario above, it goes like this. She *should* respect and honor me the way I want her to. When she doesn't, it is *awful*; I can't stand her, "the bitch." There is the *label*. She is no longer the lady he loves; she is the bitch, or worse.

Let me illustrate how sabotaging *labeling* can be. At one time I was a probation officer in San Bernardino, California. One of my first assignments was to provide supervision to a caseload of adolescent boys. I brought them to my office one at a time to get acquainted. One of the first things I noticed was all of my clients only had one name for law enforcement. They all referred to them as the "pigs." At the same time I became acquainted with several police officers. They never asked me about how the probationers were doing. They asked, "How are those little pukes doing?" So, we had the pigs and the pukes. One of our goals was to build bridges between law enforcement and our acting-out adolescents. The labeling stood in the way of any meaningful progress.

I also see this labeling process in dysfunctional families. Sometimes the family members acquire labels that hinder working together and living in harmony. The classic example is the family made up of the Bitch, the Bastard, and the Brat. The wife is no longer looked at as the woman he chose as a life partner and the woman he wants to be the mother of his children, instead she is the bitch. The husband is no longer her knight in shining amour, he is the bastard. When the parents yield to their frustration with their child's behavior, he becomes the brat. Loving roles and relationships disappear.

Family therapists often encounter this problem in families who seek counseling. The **Self-Talk** developed among family members has poisoned the whole system. They *label* each other in negative terms to the point that their conversations are void of love and acceptance.

Therapists find that *labels* given to children as they are growing up cause severe damage when the child reaches adulthood. Clients are often heard to say they were called stupid or slow to the point of believing they were incapable of doing well in school. Praise, not criticism is what children (and adults) need, especially in a family setting.

Negative, caustic *labels* dehumanize individuals.

If we want good relationships with our families, friends, and society at large, we need to talk to ourselves in a way that will allow this to happen. We are not asked to give up our preferences in life, only to understand other people have their own preferences and they see life through a different filter.

A teacher of mine, Chuck Chamberlain, wrote a book entitled, *A New Pair of Glasses*. The title is apropos, seeing things clearly is what we need to acquire if we are to keep our composure during difficult situations and difficult times. Watch out for the **shoulds**, don't **awfulize**, and drop the **labels**. I guarantee you will enjoy life more.

Summary

We have learned thoughts and beliefs that we listen to on our **Self-Talk** Tape create the feelings we experience. The feelings we create dictate our behaviors. Our behaviors keep reinforcing the **Self-Talk**. A cycle is set up as can be seen on the Self-Talk Triangle diagram. The rotating cycle does not stop. *We are in charge of the content of the tape*. That may be good news and/or that may look like bad news. The seeming bad news is that what we are experiencing, we created. The good news is if we are not completely satisfied with our creation, we can recreate it.

Remember, the three primary types of messages that cause the most trouble are:

1. We load our **Self-Talk** Tape with rigid *shoulds*. When things don't go as they *should*, we tend to

2. *Awfulize* the situation and then, we

3. *Label* things as bad or impossible and not worth working for. To one degree or another, this seems to be a human condition we are subject to. We can all do better and, when we do, everyone wins.

The Scale – the Answer to Awfulizing

I would like to introduce my readers to **The Scale** shown in the upper left hand corner of the triangle diagram (Figure 1a). Understanding this concept and how to apply it can move you to a new level of successful functioning in your life.

You will be able to keep your composure in *all* situations.

You will find no need to argue about anything.

You will be able to let others voice their opinions without feeling threatened.

You will know peace in the middle of a storm.

You will have gained the priceless commodity of tolerance.

The Scale can help us decide how big of a problem we are going to make out of any situation we encounter. **The Scale** goes from Zero to Ten with Ten representing the worst possible problem we could imagine. When I ask people to tell me the worst possible thing they could imagine, they often say it would be the death of one of their children or being diagnosed with a terminal illness with a very short time to live. Most people rate these situations as a Ten.

If such a situation happens in our life, we have a choice of how to handle it. Here is the secret. We get to decide how big any given problem is going to be by how we talk to ourselves on our **Self-Talk** Tape. Let's look at a couple of cases in point.

If you observe how relatives of a recently departed child behave at a funeral, you would see a variety of reactions. Some mourners are angry, others feel guilty; all would probably feel sad. Yet, they respond in a very different manner because they are talking to themselves differently. Some are completely despondent and unable to function. Others, while still feeling their emotions, are able to function and add to the occasion in a positive way and are able to comfort others.

By their individual **Self-Talk** each one assigns a number value to this event. Some may be saying to themselves, "I can't stand this, I can't go on living; I feel like killing myself." Others may say to themselves, "I am so sad at my loss but our baby will suffer no more pain and is in a better place. I will miss her."

One parent creates a size Four or Five response, the other a size Ten or greater. Neither parent is right or wrong with their response; they simply handle a tough situation differently by creating different **Self-Talk**.

Let me tell you about a fellow named Randy Pausch. He was an energetic young computer science professor at Carnegie Mellon, a happily married father of three, when he was diagnosed with terminal cancer that would take his life in short order. Analytical as he was, he asked himself what he was going to do with this news. He decided to not turn the problem into a Ten. Instead he developed a presentation intended for his kids, *The Last Lecture*, that he videotaped while he delivered it to his students and colleagues as a farewell.

Randy's friend collaborated with him to compile the material in book form that became a best seller in 2008 when media outlets worldwide broadcast the final lecture. Because he chose to treat the situation as less than a Ten, he inspired millions.

The Key is we get to assign a value to any problem or challenge we encounter. There are no automatic Tens in life. I encourage all my clients to describe their problems as no bigger than a Two or Three. We are in charge of our thinking. If we want to experience a more peaceful, loving, harmonious life, it is up to us.

The Scale is a valuable tool. Many of my clients report back to me when they encountered a situation during the week that they could have easily *awfulized* the problem into a Ten, but using this tool they were able to keep it at a One or Two. They felt very good about themselves and their new way of looking at their difficulties.

How Do We Change Self-Talk?

You may be saying, "OK, I'm convinced. I understand the power of **Self-Talk**. Now, how can I change it to better serve my needs and create a better world for myself and for all those I care about?" While this is a question with more than one simple answer, I can offer some approaches that will help.

First, let's go back to The Triangle. We now see clearly that whatever we listen to on our Self-Talk Tape creates the feelings we experience.

Thoughts create feelings.

Feelings dictate behaviors.

Our behaviors reinforce the existing thoughts on our Self-Talk Tape.

When our thoughts and **Self-Talk** generate anger, that anger cycles around the triangle creating our experience. The same is true if we generate thoughts of peace, cooperation, harmony, and kindness.

Self-Talk creates my world.

Understanding this, we can start changing the content of our **Self-Talk** at any corner of the Triangle. Some people need to focus on changing behaviors. As we implement and practice new healthier behaviors, change occurs. Alcoholics Anonymous is a good example of how this works. When a newcomer arrives at his/her first meeting, he/she will often meet an old-timer who will give some firm direction, "Just sit down, shut up, and listen." While this may at first seem harsh, if followed, the newcomer will start to experience a change in his/her **Self-Talk.**

Self-Talk's old messages of hopelessness will be supplanted by new messages of hope. By sitting down, shutting up, and listening he/she will begin to see how others have been able to conquer the drink problem. Messages of personal hope begin to develop as the newcomer listens to other stories of recovery. This generates change in the newcomer's behavior. A new behavioral pattern usually takes at least three weeks to establish and to start feeling like normal behavior. It may take longer to change but it is well worth the effort.

Some of us need to approach change at the corner of the Triangle labeled **Feelings**. Some people may need medication or medical attention before they address changes in their behavior. Medical attention may be a part of an ongoing plan of change.

Suicidal, seriously depressed, and agitated persons may be helped by psychiatric and medical care. Emotions that are completely out of control are best attended to before and while behavioral change is being implemented. Look at our homeless population on skid row and in our institutions. If many of them were appropriately medicated, they could tend to the rest of their lives and could return to productive living.

Your change can begin by starting at any corner of the triangle. Real progress begins when we address our thoughts.

Counseling

Counseling as an approach to change takes many forms. Some forms help people regress in time to help them understand how they became the persons they are today. By uncovering childhood issues, sometimes it's easier to see how thinking patterns developed into what they are today. As children we were like tape recorders storing messages in our memory bank that we received from others, memories that are both productive and destructive. We didn't evaluate the messages as children because our brains were not fully developed. As adults we have an opportunity and an obligation to ourselves to evaluate what we have learned and change the messages that no longer work for us.

Another form of counseling known as Rational, Emotive, Behavioral Therapy (REBT) is particularly valuable. This is a treatment model developed by the late Dr. Albert Ellis. Many variations of this model are also helpful. REBT can be particularly helpful in addressing the three destructive thought patterns discussed above. Many therapists specialize in some form of cognitive behavioral therapy including REBT. There are numerous workbooks that can also help people systematically dismantle and restructure their belief system and train themselves, with or without the help of a counselor, to change their Self-Talk.

If you are completely stuck in your life and feel a need to talk it out, don't hesitate to seek out a well trained and experienced counselor or therapist to help start a rewarding change experience. However, if you do not have overwhelming issues in your life that need to be worked through, let me introduce you to another excellent method of changing your Self-Talk.

Coaching

Life Coaching is a relatively new discipline that can be extremely helpful in getting a person to see how they sabotage their own efforts at creating the world they would like to live in.

Coaching starts where counseling usually stops. Too often people find themselves frustrated with their lives. By listening to their Self-Talk, they have convinced themselves there is no hope for a better future. Life seems to go nowhere and they don't know where to turn. They need someone to be their guide as they clarify who they really are and show them that they are capable of great things, contrary to what they have been telling themselves.

Just as a football coach does not go out onto the field, a Life Coach does not enter into the client's life. The Life Coach helps the player understand his/her strengths and capabilities, and helps the player see how he or she may have been limiting themselves. Coaches help the players uncover life-long intentions that may have been buried for years and assist in developing goals to achieve them. Like the football coach, the Life Coach works with the player to challenge and support with the intention to help the player be the very best he or she can be. Then, they walk with the players on their journey. ***This is powerful work in changing Self-Talk.***

Religion

Many people find solace in religion. Teachings developed over centuries provide answers to life and give a guideline on how they can conduct their lives. Theological and ethical beliefs help a person add structure to his/her life and provide a sense of safety that offer rewards in this life and the next. Structured religion also adds a strong sense of camaraderie, knowing that thousands believe as they believe. Religion also often gives us a sense of mission; feed and clothe the poor, spread the gospel (literally: the good news) to all corners of the earth.

However, when learned beliefs turn into rigid dogma, discomfort can arise. Belief systems have to be defended in family, community and internationally when they are dogmatic. The Self-Talk stating, "My beliefs are right and all others are wrong" brings more unhappiness and disharmony than can be tolerated. At that point, many find it necessary to examine their Self-Talk to see if it brings the joy and productivity they desire.

Again, Self-Talk creates the world of the individual. When people have connected with new church teachings that encourage thoughts of love, kindness, peace, forgiveness, and harmony, their thoughts will create corresponding feelings. These feelings will dictate kind and loving behaviors that reinforce the original thoughts. ***The cycle around the triangle is always in play.***

Changing Self-Talk from a religious perspective remains the same. If you are happy, joyous, and free, and life is what you want it to be, you will enjoy and continue to create a loving, beautiful, harmonious world for yourself and the world at large. The world needs as many of us with these qualities as it can get.

Support Groups
Another very effective way to modify Self-Talk is with the help of self-help groups. Self-help groups come in a variety of forms. One of the oldest and most effective is Alcoholics Anonymous (AA). Based on twelve suggested spiritual steps, several million people have turned their lives around. It is worth spending a little time to better understand how the AA program, and programs like it, work.

Twelve Step programs are designed to help people overcome serious addiction problems. There is nothing like an addiction to create negative self-defeating thoughts. As people enter recovery they have often put themselves and the people they love through an emotional wringer. They have had to justify errant and hurtful behaviors. They have developed Self-Talk about their guilt and shame; they blame, get angry, and sometimes are depressed to the point of suicide.

By participating in the fellowship of AA and working the steps, they are able to start talking to themselves differently. In so doing, the feelings about themselves, others, and life have changed. Learned and practiced new behaviors support a new way of thinking. The triangle cycles the thought, feelings, and behaviors.

Spirituality

Many of us have had religious teachings that we have rejected, others have never had any religious teachings. Some people may not have been given a meaningful set of precepts to follow. Others have strayed from early teachings and have feelings of being lost in the far country. People introduced to spiritual tenets, find the spiritual path needs to be lived and practiced in order to bring the rewards in life that they seek. They discover a need to examine their beliefs and Self-Talk, and clean house, getting rid of old Self-Talk that is not producing the results they want. Many come to the conclusion that as Socrates pointed out, "The unexamined life is not worth living."

One's spiritual path is a personal, experiential path. It is going inside for answers rather than looking for answers others provide. It is a path of questioning, and standing in awe of the answers that are revealed. It is a path that allows a person to know that he/she is one with all that is. They begin to enjoy a whole new quality of Self-Talk.

There are a great many gurus and teachers who will tell you how and what to believe. The better ones will encourage you to go within to find your answers and will walk with you on that journey.

My teacher and mentor, Dr. Herbert Beierle, teaches that Self-Talk is the key to the good life making you the true creator of your world. When I dwell only on the positive there is no room for the negative. When I see myself as the creator of my world, I am truly free. Through meditation and affirmations my world becomes a delightful place to live.

Wayne Dyer likes to tell the story of calling his friend Deepak Chopra for an answer to a problem. Deepak's solution is always the same, "…meditate."

How do we change Self-Talk? There are myriad ways. However you decide to approach it, remember that you are changing your world. It can be an exciting, rewarding and exhilarating endeavor. If you choose to proceed, I applaud you.

Changing our attitude about ourselves and life can be helped by all the approaches we have previously discussed. A Therapist/Counselor can help us reframe our thoughts and the way we talk. A Life Coach can help us identify and stay true to our life intention of finding peace of mind. Seeking a religious stance that is loving and kind can help immensely. Jesus said, "Love your neighbor as yourself." If we really did that, think of the difference it would create on our Self-Talk Tape. Spiritually, coming to know that we are all created equal and that the Spirit of God resides in each of us, will create massive change.

Try these techniques. You deserve the best life possible!

Summary

We have demonstrated how thoughts (Self-Talk) create feelings that we act out in our behaviors and that how we act reinforces our thoughts. Also provided are some effective ways to start the self-examination process that will result in positive change. My hope is that if you are struggling with the trials of life, you will give yourself the opportunity to turn your focus around and allow yourself to see beyond the delusion that everything is bad and that your situation (whatever it is) is hopeless. Whatever you focus on will increase and enlarge. ***It really is up to you.***

Healthy Self-Talk

In order to create our world through Self-Talk we need to know what healthy, vital, effective Self-Talk is. I know every person, place, and thing in my world is created by the way I talk to myself. When I encounter my wife each day, I create her in my world. If I tell myself that she is the most loving, beautiful, fantastic person, then she is…in my world. If I tell myself that I love my job, that it provides a means to take care of my family's needs, and it is a place where I can be of service to others, then it is so…in my world. If I tell myself I am a capable, loving, fantastic person, then I am… in my world.

Frequently I see bumper stickers citing Jesus that reads, "Not of this world, but in it." Could that mean that while I live as a vital functioning human being IN this world, I am not OF it? The world I create through my thoughts is a whole new reality. I don't need to deny the physical realm. In fact, I want to deal with issues as they arise. When challenges present themselves whether they be physical, financial, or relational I want to take care them.

How I take care of life's challenges depends on my Self-Talk. I can look at a challenge and become mesmerized or obsessed by it. I can tell myself this challenge rates Ten on the scale we discussed earlier. I can worry, fret, and fall into hopelessness and despair. ***Awfulizing*** creates a negative experience in my world. By my own thinking I can become emotionally paralyzed.

I can look at the same challenge knowing it is a situation in the physical world and it does not change my inner reality. I can still tell myself I am a capable, loving, fantastic person. I can weigh it out on my scale (see the diagram in the front of the book, Figure 1a) and assign a much lower number to the seriousness of the situation. When we practice a new way of talking to ourselves, we can walk through any situation with focus, clarity, ease, and grace.

It truly is simple when I keep the triangle in mind. How I talk to myself (my **thoughts**) creates the **feelings** I experience which dictate how I **behave**.

I personally benefit from practicing positive, effective, loving Self-Talk. I use or have used many of the tools mentioned. I meditate and practice affirmative prayer (affirmations). I read positive, life-affirming books and I surround myself with people who are supportive and who are like-minded positive thinkers. I work and try to share all that I find positive with those I meet. I practice forgiveness of others and self. In other words, I **work** at making friends with my thoughts. Interestingly, the more I **work** at it, the more **fun** it is.

It works; it really does, and the more you do it the better you get. Practice makes perfect. When you clear away old negative messages embedded on your Self-Talk Tape and replace them with positive messages you will know a new freedom and quality of life that you never knew existed.

Education vs. Application

I have always believed there is a difference between education and application. If you have read this far, you have been introduced to concepts that may work well for you. The question now is how does one apply these concepts in daily life?

My daughter, Cindy, suggested that I create a workbook to help in this endeavor. I resist the term *work*book and choose to see this section as a *play*book. As a football coach develops a playbook for any eventuality that may develop on the field, I believe we can benefit by developing our own life playbook. When situations in life arise we respond with Self-Talk triggered by the messages that we have allowed to inhabit our Self-Talk Tape. We might ask ourselves if we have done the work to clean up our tape so that we do not make situations into Eights, Nines and Tens on our *awfulization* scale. Let's look at some specific situations that are frequently difficult to handle.

Relationships

We stand in relationship with every other person on earth, living and dead. There are people in the physical world and people who reside in my consciousness. There are people I live with, those who I interact with daily and those I see on television or some other media. There are those that shape the physical world in which I live (both domestic and foreign). There are those that make up my heritage, my parents and grandparents and people in my community, teachers, preachers, and so on.

I stand in relation to all of these people because I have thoughts about them. They are frequently the content of my Self-Talk. The way I Self-Talk create *feelings* I experience which dictates my *behaviors* toward them and my behavior as a whole. When I tell myself how they *should* act or *should* have acted but didn't, I create feelings that are not pleasant and I tend to act badly. The good news is if I drop *should* thoughts I will experience peace of mind and will be able to act appropriately with a sense of ease and integrity.

I have a friend who talks about his relatives as the "goddamn loved ones." He chooses to live on one coast while his relatives live on the opposite coast. He uses this label and description in an attempt to be humorous and possibly to divert the pain he feels for not having the close relationship he would truly like to have.

As a therapist, I have worked with countless clients who describe their significant others in angry, unforgiving ways. For themselves they create a lot of pain by *awfulizing* the behaviors of others, "They should have treated me better and it is *awful* they didn't." *Awfulizing* makes it easy to *label* them as rotten relatives and friends. In their mind, they become backstabbers or worse.

Some of the worse labeling we direct toward the persons closest to us, "My parents screwed up my life," or, "My spouse is a cheater and liar." Another statement might be, "My children are driving me crazy; they are rotten kids." How am I to achieve peaceful, loving feelings when my Self-Talk is loaded with negative messages? Often people will say the negative judgments are the truth. When I hear that statement, I know it is true for that person at that moment. Changing Self-Talk is imperative *if* you want different results.

Let's look at the *play*book. When I realize that what I have been doing has not brought me joy or happiness and my life's intention is to live at peace with others, the first step is to learn to live at peace with my own head. I need to create Self-Talk messages that bring feelings I desire. Even simple changes can make a difference. Here is an example:

Old Message	*A Better Message*	*The Best Message*
My parents screwed up my life	My parents could have done much better, but they probably did the best they could	My parents are God's kids just like me. I forgive and release them to their own good so that I may seek mine

In coaching this would be deemed a great play, because it works and it brings desired results. My parents don't need to change in order for me to be free; my thoughts about them need to change. Putting great messages in our *play*book makes life a winning game.

Relationship to Self

We have been discussing our relationships with others which can sometimes be challenging. But there is another relationship that is equally challenging and that is our relationship with self. If you are like most folks you are constantly evaluating your own thoughts, feelings, and behaviors. The Self-Talk in this department is almost non-stop.

I *should* have spoken up. I should have kept my mouth shut. How **should** I have acted? I am too tall, short, fat or thin. I **should** have gone to college. I **should** have married or stayed single. **Should** I take that other job or **should** I stay put? I **should** be more successful. On and on it goes;

it seems to never stop. About the only time we are not evaluating ourselves is when we are taking the inventory of someone else. So, not only do we ***should*** all over other people, we also ***should*** all over ourselves.

All of this ***shoulding*** or self-monitoring happens on our Self-Talk Tape. We know that whatever is happening in our Self-Talk creates the feelings we experience and these feelings dictate our actions. It behooves us to be aware of what we listen to and change the messages so we can experience peace.

It is only as we become aware of what we do to ourselves that we can change.

Learning to love, forgive, and honor ourselves is key to developing positive Self-Talk. When I look upon my world, I need to see myself as worthy as any of God's kids. When I come to that realization, I can be one of, rather than feeling apart from, all others.

We can also set ourselves apart from others by being prideful. When I treat others badly to make myself feel superior, I sabotage my efforts to develop the Self-Talk that will bring harmony and good feelings to my life.

Events

Life continues to present challenges. We may wonder how we are to react to events in our lives that appear to be catastrophes. We have a choice of how to respond. Issues regarding health, finances, relationships, and community occur. Stuff happens. If we have not done the work on our Tape that allows us to respond with equanimity we experience emotional discomfort and sometimes emotional terror.

If we are not prepared, events in our lives can create a response of Nine or Ten on our awfulization scale. Having learned how all-important the Self-Talk Triangle is, we can challenge old messages that are no longer of any use and replace them with messages that allow us to create feelings and actions that are more harmonious, positive, and life-affirming.

In my work and in my personal life, I observe how people handle the news of serious illness, death, financial ruin, loss of a home or job and other major events. It is fascinating how people react. I was part of a welcoming home group for soldiers returning from Iraq. I talked with dozens of them. I expected all of them to be joyous about coming home. To my surprise, many of them wanted to return immediately to the war zone. That is where they felt the most comfortable and the most useful. I heard statements like, "That is where I belong, with my buddies. I understand the war zone but I have difficulty handling my home life, my wife, and kids. Fighting the bad guys is my job and I just want to do my job." I have come to believe that an individual's response or reaction is a result of how they talk to themselves about the event. ***It is not what happens to us so much as how we talk to ourselves about what happened.***

A Personal Toolkit for Change

We have seen so far how the Self-Talk Triangle works. The thoughts I entertain create the feelings that dictate my behavior. We understand that there are three primary ways that our Self-Talk sabotages our goal of living a joyous, fulfilling life and living in harmony with ourselves and others. We have learned about many venues where help is available to change our Self-Talk. We have identified specific areas of application for the things we are learning. Now I would like to offer specific proven tools to bring about the desired change.

Acceptance

Acceptance is the starting point of all forward progress. When I accept what is, rather than demanding what should be, I can move on. As I am writing this, I think of President Obama and the situation he faces as he assumes office. To be able to make plans to move our country forward he needs to understand and **accept** where the country is.

Acceptance does not mean approval. Acceptance means to survey the situation and to get real about the circumstances as they are. Acceptance is a tool to get realistically focused on the now. Accepting you, me, and the situation exactly as it is begins the change process.

Perhaps the best statement I have seen regarding acceptance comes from the literature of Alcoholics Anonymous.

Alcoholics Anonymous, Third Edition, 1976
Page 449

"And acceptance is the answer to all my problems today. When I am disturbed, it is because I find some person, place, thing, or situation – some fact of my life – unacceptable to me, and I can find no serenity until I accept that person, place, thing or situation as being exactly the way it is suppose to be at this moment. Nothing, absolutely nothing, happens in God's world by mistake. Until I could accept my alcoholism, I could not stay sober; unless I accept life completely on life's terms, I cannot be happy. I need to concentrate not so much on what needs to be changed in the world as on what needs to be changed in me."

Remember, acceptance does not mean approval. What I need to accept as my current reality may not meet with my approval. But, at least I am clear about my starting point for change.

Thought Stopping

As hard as we try to prevent it, negative thoughts still seem to appear on our Self-Talk Tape. They usually come as left-over messages from years of old social conditioning. The message we were given as children by our caretakers became our truth until we became mature enough to challenge it and change the messages that don't work. These messages seem to come automatically, such as:

- I can't do that.
- It's too hard.
- Why try?
- Life sucks.
- He/She is such a jerk.

What can we do when these thoughts appear? If you are aware of the negative thought, then it shows that you have learned a lot from your studies in this book. Many people live on automatic pilot and have no awareness of their thoughts, let alone the awareness that they can change them.

When I am aware that I am drifting into negativity, I need to stop that thought on the spot. I tell myself, "Stop; don't go there." Sometimes I will become a little dramatic and say out loud, "Shut up, Steckdaub." Other times a gentle reminder suffices.

We can stop the flow of thoughts and channel them in a different direction. It is equally important to shift our attention and focus on something else. "Refocus," says my wife the coach. I can refocus by becoming visually aware of my surroundings. "Where am I? What am I doing and where am I going?" Have you ever been driving on the freeway, lost in thought and missed your turnoff? When it happens, we stop the thought and refocus. The same thing happens when we become aware of negative thoughts that we nurture. ***We stop the thought and refocus.***

Practice refocusing daily. You will become the master of your own thoughts. Living consciously (conscious of your thoughts, actions, and desires, etc.) is truly the mature and effective way to live. It is the opposite of the way many of us have been accustomed to living our lives.

Here's an important caveat. All of these suggestions and instructions are valuable only ***IF*** you want to change. ***IF*** you do not really want to bring about change and improve the quality of your life, then you might consider this interesting reading but far too much work to tackle. As I have studied and practiced these simple concepts in my own life, I have found them to be straightforward but not necessarily easy. Nevertheless, the more I apply the principles the more fulfilling my life becomes.

Reframing and Affirmations

Reframing and affirmations are valuable tools. When I become aware of a negative thought, and remove the negativity, I am able to see it in a different light. Negative thoughts are framed in negative words. Listed below are examples of reframing:

Old Frame	**New Frame**
My dog died and I can't imagine living without him.	My dog died and I will really miss him, yet I am so grateful for the years we had together

One frame brings pain and sadness, the other brings a level of acceptance. One frame brings a heaviness that can interfere with our functioning and the other allows us to experience a sense of joy and gratitude while we move through the experience.

Feeling the feelings of loss are natural when we walk through a difficult experience. When we put a frame around these feelings and hang the frame on the wall to stare at all day long, our suffering can become intense and debilitating. When we work at catching ourselves and practice reframing our ***thoughts***, we experience less ***feelings*** of emotional pain and our ***behaviors*** can return to normal more quickly.

Using affirmations is another valuable tool in creating the world in which we wish to live. When I form a habit of consistently affirming the good or the best in *every* situation, life becomes a very different and gratifying experience. I listened to an interview recently of Louise Hay, a marvelous New Thought teacher and healer. No matter what she was asked by the interviewer her responses were always positive. She spoke only in positive terms about herself and about every person and situation that was brought into the conversation.

Practicing reframing and affirmations also works well in the field of creating prosperity. When we learn to reframe our old thinking and use affirmations appropriately great things can happen. I highly recommend the books by Catherine Ponder as a reference of how to create affirmations and use them to create abundance in every area of you life.

Forgiveness

One of the greatest tools you can put in your toolkit is forgiveness. As a result of forgiving, you release the other person (or institution) from your negative thought bank. It is a process of letting go. Holding on tight to an object for too long becomes very uncomfortable. We tend to become tired or even exhausted from holding on. The moment we let go, we can relax.

The same is true with forgiveness. When we hold on to an old emotional wound or hurt, we tire and are less efficient. It becomes more difficult to focus on the now. When we hold resentment of another person, it is as if we are letting someone live in our head rent free.

Forgiving does not necessarily involve forgetting. When the remembrance of the event that hurt you occurs, apply everything you have learned in this book. Acknowledge the unforgiving message you created on your Self-Talk Tape. Remember, the longer you hold on to the message and the more you re-play it over and over in your head, the stronger it gets. It will create *feelings* and *behaviors* that you don't want to experience.

To master your Self-Talk Tape, let the negativity go. Reframe the thought. Rather than thinking, "That rotten so and so, I hate him/her." You can reframe by saying, "I forgive him/her. I don't approve of what he/she said or did <u>and</u> I let go." Personally, I like the concept of giving him/her back to God, "God, he's your kid, you deal with him."

Remember the goal is to free your Self-Talk from any negativity. Create anew your perception of the problem (or situation). "I want to be free, so I drop the burden. I let go and let God."

Indeed, if you truly want to clear the Self-Talk Tape, begin wishing the other person every good thing that you would wish for yourself. Remember, forgiveness is not about the other person; it is about your peace of mind. When a thought of the offender comes into your stream of consciousness, bless him, wish him well, and refocus your thoughts on something more positive. Try this technique for thirty days and watch your world change.

Another aspect of forgiveness is forgiveness of self. It is a prerequisite for achieving peace of mind. How am I ever to find peace and happiness when I am constantly thinking badly of myself? I have heard people say, "If anyone would have treated me the way I have treated myself, I would have wanted to kill them."

If we want to create a new world of experience for ourselves, we need to let go of the old. My friend Claudia Black is fond of talking about "gunny sacking" our feelings. We throw the feeling in a gunnysack and carry it around with us rather than feeling the feeling, forgiving, and letting it go. The sack can get heavy and become a deterrent to experiencing the good life.

Gratitude

An old timer told me once, "Thems that's grateful are happy. Thems that's not are not." It's true. Grateful people are happy people. The happiest people I know are truly grateful for what they have in life in spite of the consequences. They are people who have a rich inner life and are not waiting for some external source to solve all of their problems.

We are narrow and limited when we can only focus on the things that seem to go wrong. This is a big world both in the inside spiritual dimension and in the external physical universe. There is always something for which we can be grateful if only we look.

I have a cousin in her late seventies, who can barely move sometimes from her arthritic condition, yet I never see her without a smile on her face. She is so grateful for what she has in her heart and in her home that she has very little time to focus on what she does not have. She is an inspiration to everyone. She is so busy giving of herself that she rarely acknowledges the constant pain she feels. That is gratitude in action.

By applying the tools offered in this book, you will have what a teacher of mine calls, "a new pair of glasses." You will be able to view people, places, things, and events differently. In so doing you will develop new messages of gratitude for your Self-Talk Tape.

When I live in gratitude, I live fully in the present. I am constantly looking for the good in any situation so I can feel gratitude.

As I write this I am sitting snow-bound in Cheyenne, Wyoming where I am on a consulting assignment with the United States Air Force, working with Airmen and their families as they adjust to war-time living. It is cold and I am missing my family and my home in Southern California. And, I am grateful! I am grateful for the privilege of being here to help where I can. I am grateful for the health I have that enables me to do the work I love. I am grateful for my wife who supports me and keeps the home fires burning. I am grateful for my friends and family.

Now, what do I want to listen to on my Self-Talk Tape? Do I want to listen to complaints about cold weather or do I want to listen to reminders of all I have to be grateful for? I challenge you right now to set this book aside and write a list of twenty things for which you are grateful. You will feel great. The more you focus on gratitude, the better you will feel.

Summary

Try working with these tools. They are time tested and proven to work. To the degree that you apply them to your life, you will experience change.

Reframe situations. Don't sit around stewing about how bad everyone and everything is. When you are constantly talking about the negative, you are not only bringing yourself down but you are affecting everyone around you. Your negativity will affect every relationship, every business deal, and will even affect your health. You may even wonder why positive people are shunning you and other negative people are seeking you out; like seeks like.

Affirm. Use affirmations even if you feel they are of no benefit. You are programming your mind to talk in positive terms. The effort will bear fruit. You will be putting messages on your Self-Talk Tape that brings feelings you want to experience and that bring you joy. Some people curse the chatter in their head. If you practice the tools in this book, you will take charge of the chatter and make it work on your behalf.

Refocus your thinking away from your problems when they enter your consciousness. You can't always be in control of your thinking but the more you practice with these tools, the more your thinking will naturally be on a higher plane. Your automatic responses will be more positive and hopeful. You will be the master of your thoughts rather than be their slave. What freedom you will have.

Forgive. When I forgive, I set myself free. I no longer need to spend my time mulling over old events that have little to do with today, with this moment. The way he acted, is the way he acted. What she said, she said. What I did, I did. If amends are in order, make them. Forgive and set yourself free from the past. Get on with your present and your future. If you have trouble in this area, go back and re-read the section on Education vs. Application beginning on page 22. Apply the tools from your religion; apply the twelve steps if this is your program of support. Use your coach or counselor and the tools they offer to help you with your journey.

Express ***gratitude***. Act grateful. Show your gratitude by being quick to help others. Support those who support you, financially and in any other way you can. Compliment constantly. Be quick to praise others. Stop complaining. This new focused attitude and action will bring a multitude of blessings. Your Self-Talk will no longer be focused on what can I get but rather on what can I give.

Get real. Accept what is at this moment. If you have a troubled marriage or faltering career, accept it as troubled at this moment. It is what it is. Don't deny it. Now you can see the issue more clearly and you can develop a plan to deal with it. Know that life moves forward, never backward. With these tools you can better chart your path to a future that you never dreamed possible.

Self-Talk Worksheet

Assess your current perception of what you feel right now.

I feel (mad, sad, glad, etc.)_____

_____

My Self-Talk says:_____ **should** _____

_____

(Example: He/she or I **should**, my boss **should**, my spouse **should** etc.)

What would I like to happen:_____

_____

_____

_____

What would it take for this to happen?_____

_____

_____

_____

Things I could do right now are: _____

_____

_____

_____

I will change my Self-Talk in the following ways ***starting right now.***

> I will reframe the situation to emphasize the positive.
>
> I will create and practice positive affirmations so I can stay positive.
>
> I will practice dismissing any negative thought regarding this situation.
>
> I will practice acceptance and forgiveness.
>
> I will maintain a gratitude list for all of the blessings I have in my life.

A Personal Action Plan

Changing our Self-Talk in order to live a beautiful, fulfilling life may take some work. If by reading this book, you have been inspired to make some personal changes, give this action plan a thirty day trial. Just be willing. Willingness is the key to change.

1. Start your day with these five specific affirmative statements. Say them with meaning and sincerity. Repeat them several times during the day.

    • I am a child of God and deserve all of His blessings.

    • I will treat *every* person today with the same respect I expect from others.

    • I will focus on the abundance in my life and give thanks.

    • I will be the best person I can today.

    • I like me.

2. Create a visual in your mind. Picture yourself at the end of your day relaxing in your favorite chair. Affirm that it has been a good day. Name three things you did well. Think of at least one incident which you could have awfulized a situation into a

high number on the scale but you were able to keep the number to a One or Two. Name three things you would like to improve in your thoughts and behaviors tomorrow.

3. Start a gratitude list. Each day add three things to your list for which you are grateful. They can be large or small things. When you enter gratitude, mean it, feel it, be sincere. Review your entire list each night before you go to bed. After thirty days you will have a list of ninety things for which you are grateful. It is hard to continue negative Self-Talk when you fill yourself with gratitude.

4. Read some devotional literature every day. If you belong to a religious organization, they can provide you with appropriate literature. Twelve Step programs have daily readings. You can also find such material on-line. An excellent source is The Daily Word and can be found at WWW.Unity.Com.

Try these four steps for thirty days. We do not need to be controlled by our undisciplined thinking. Experience and enjoy the change.

God bless you (and I bless you) as you take charge of your Self-Talk and create the world in which you would like to live. I would like to leave you with a wonderful quote.

What can I do to heal myself?
"To heal I have a consistent thought about myself. The truth about myself is that my body, my mind and my affairs are in perfect order right now. God has created everything perfect and therefore I am perfect. It might appear that I have a problem, but it is not my divine reality. *To experience my perfection I have to change my thinking and my attitude about myself, my family and my world.* In every moment I speak my word:

- I like me
- I am whole and perfect
- I live in my eternally perfect body Every Organ, Action, Function of my body is whole and perfect right now
- I am surrounded by harmonious beings
- I am independently wealthy
- All is in divine order

Dr. Herbert L. Beierle
Dean and Founder
University of Healing
Campo, CA

About the Author

Don Steckdaub lives with his wife, Rita, and two puppies in Murrieta, California. He has worked in the counseling field for more than forty years. He is a licensed marriage family therapist and a certified alcohol and drug abuse counselor. He has earned a master's degree in marriage and family therapy and doctorate degrees in psychology and philosophy.

He has worked in all areas of addiction treatment and has consulted with numerous corporations creating and supervising treatment programs. He has worked closely with county probation and the courts, creating programs for domestic violence, child abuse and sexual offenses. He has worked in private practice specializing in marital issues and has worked for the past seven years as a military and family life consultant.

Visit his website *YourthoughtsCreate.com*.

Printed in the United States
By Bookmasters